Pink Pretty Thoughts

A collection of positive thoughts inspired by Instagram posts.

compiled by Keryl Pesce

Pink Pretty Thoughts

Images from dreamstime.com, Pixabay and Keryl Pesce.

Published by Little Pink Press, P.O. Box 847, Beacon, NY 12508.

ISBN: 978-0692910276

This book is dedicated to
the part of you that knows just
how amazing you really are.

Thank you to the following for being part
of this project.

@imdeborahhanlon
@jeannekellycredit
@jonna_spilbor
@pinupmakeover
@soulsistercoaching
@thechampagnediet
@thecreativepotential

Last but not least.
My Muse

#bekind

KINDNESS

is an antidepressant

HOW YOU MAKE
others feel says
A LOT ABOUT WHO YOU ARE.

@kerylpesce

In a world full of "look at me" girls, be a "come with me" girl.

-Cara Alwill Leyba

The effect you have

on others is the most valuable

currency there is.

-Jim Carrey

—— WHEN ——
YOU SEE SOMETHING

beautiful

IN SOMEONE,
SAY IT.

@KERYLPESCE

YOU HAVE THE

magical

POWER

TO LEAVE OTHERS FEELING
BETTER THAN YOU FOUND THEM.

——— USE IT. ———

@KERYLPESCE

Wake up.
Kick ass.
Be kind.
Repeat.

@soulsistercoaching

YOUR GREATEST
ACHIEVEMENTS WILL BE
THE ROLE
YOU PLAY IN
HELPING OTHERS
ACHIEVE THEIR DREAMS
AND FULFILL THEIR
DESTINIES.
AND IN DOING SO, YOU WILL
HAVE FULFILLED YOURS.
-KERYL PESCE

#believe

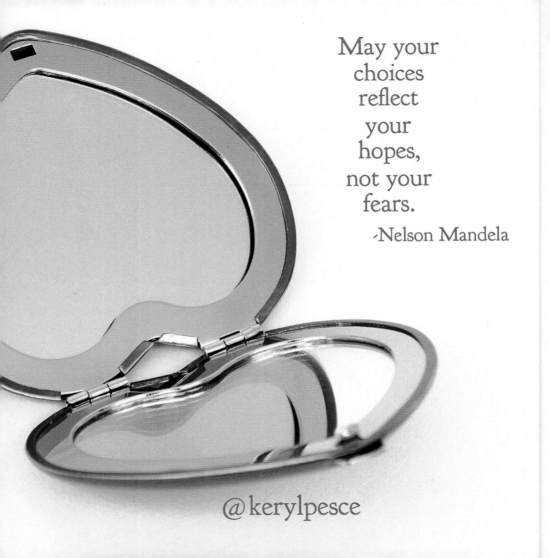

May your
choices
reflect
your
hopes,
not your
fears.

-Nelson Mandela

@kerylpesce

CHIN UP
BEAUTIFUL

@KERYLPESCE

SOMETIMES YOU NEED
TO SEE IT TO BELIEVE IT,
AND SOMETIMES YOU NEED
TO BELIEVE IT TO SEE IT.

@imdeborahhanlon

BELIEVE
IN YOU

I believe that
happy girls
are the prettiest girls.

-Audrey Hepburn

@kerylpesce

BELIEVE IN THE

Goodness of others.

@KERYLPESCE

When
the universe starts
lining things up for
you in
a way that no human mind could ever do,
it will take your breath away.

-Rhonda Byrne

@kerylpesce

Every
day holds
the possibility
of a miracle.

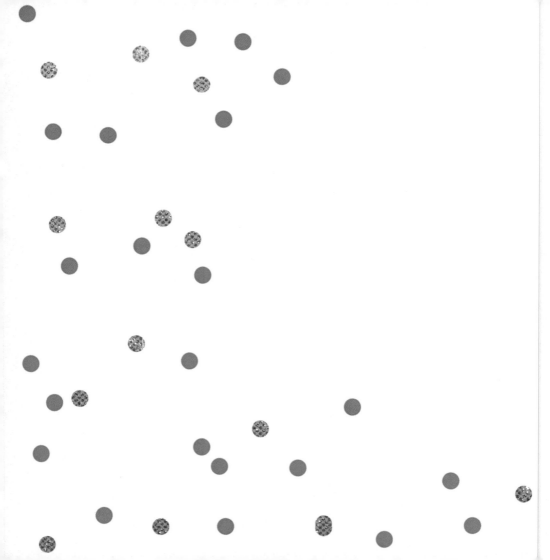

#happiness

Happiness is a state of mind,
not a state of circumstance.

SHE WENT ON

A DATE WITH

HAPPINESS

AND

FELL IN LOVE

@KERYLPESCE

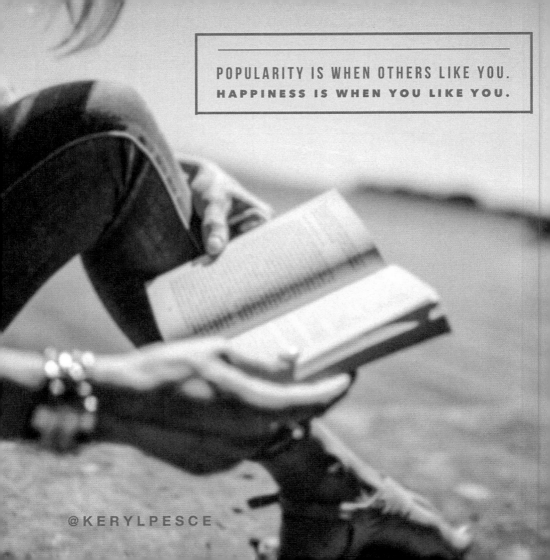

POPULARITY IS WHEN OTHERS LIKE YOU.
HAPPINESS IS WHEN YOU LIKE YOU.

@KERYLPESCE

I AM MY
HAPPY PLACE.

SUCCESS IS NOT THE KEY TO HAPPINESS. HAPPINESS IS THE KEY TO SUCCESS.

-ALBERT SCHWEITZER

@KERYLPESCE

DOING

something that makes you

HAPPY IS AN ACT

of kindness for your soul.

@kerylpesce

FOLLOW

YOUR

SMILE

@KERYLPESCE

Happiness comes when you stop letting things you can't control, control you.

@kerylpesce

#doyou

Beauty begins
the moment you decide
to be yourself.
-Coco Chanel

@kerylpesce

SURROUND
yourself with
PEOPLE WHO GET YOU

@SOULSISTERCOACHING

Self
confidence
   is hands
down,
   the most
beautiful,
   sexy feature a
   woman can have.

-Keryl Pesce, "Happy Bitch"

IF YOU ARE ALWAYS TRYING TO BE NORMAL YOU WILL
NEVER KNOW HOW AMAZING YOU CAN BE.
•-MAYA ANGELOU•

She doesn't need
to have it all together
to have it all.

@thecreativepotential

I may not
be perfect,
but I'm a perfect me.

BE YOURSELF.
THE WORLD WORSHIPS
THE ORIGINAL.
-INGRID BERGMAN

@PINUPMAKEOVER

THERE IS NO WRONG WAY TO BE YOURSELF.

-CARA ALWILL LEYBA

#havefaith

Hardships often
prepare ordinary
people for an
extraordinary destiny

C.S. Lewis

@kerylpesce

Be grateful for your struggles for
they give birth to your dreams.

@kerylpesce

WHEN ONE
DOOR CLOSES, ANOTHER
OPENS, BUT THE
HALLWAY IS ALWAYS A
BITCH

@KERYLPESCE

FAITH

is the new

BLACK

The best kind of faith to have is faith in yourself.

And in her darkness,

she discovered her light.

@kerylpesce

#lovelife

WHAT
YOU REALLY WANT
TO DO
IS WHAT
YOU ARE MEANT TO DO.

@KERYLPESCE

LOVE

the life you're in

@KERYLPESCE

When things don't add up,
start subtracting.

@jonna_spilbor

The only way to do great
work is to love what you do.
-Steve Jobs

@kerylpesce

YOU HAVE TO FIND WHAT

sparks a light

IN YOU SO THAT YOU IN

your own way can illuminate

THE WORLD.

-OPRAH WINFREY

@kerylpesce

MAKE IT
POP
LIKE
PINK
CHAMPAGNE

LOVE
THIS
MOMENT

@KERYLPESCE

CHOOSE A JOB
YOU LOVE,
AND YOU WILL
NEVER HAVE
TO WORK
A DAY IN YOUR LIFE.
- CONFUCIUS

selflove

It is
not
selfish
to do
what
is best
for you.
-Mark Sutton

@kerylpesce

SEE THE BEAUTY IN EVERYTHING. START WITH YOU.

HAVE YOUR OWN BACK

@kerylpesce

You can't
truly
take care of
another
until
you
first
take care
of you.

@kerylpesce

IF WE REALLY

LOVE

OURSELVES,
EVERYTHING IN
OUR LIFE WORKS.
-LOUISE HAY

@KERYLPESCE

TO DO

BE PATIENT
WITH MYSELF TODAY

WE CAN'T HATE OURSELVES INTO A

version of ourselves

WE CAN LOVE.

-LORI DESCHENE

@kerylpesce

My job is to love myself,
not judge myself.

Hello my friend.
It is my wish that in some way,
this book helps you see
the best in
you and your life
and sparks a glimpse
of what's possible for you.
There are so many reasons
to smile.
You are one of them.

I invite you to stop by and visit me
whenever you like at www.kerylpesce.com.

Much love,

Keryl

Made in the USA
Coppell, TX
02 April 2021

52936073R00045